THIS IS ME!

TREASURED POEMS

Edited By Jenni Harrison

First published in Great Britain in 2022 by:

Young Writers
Remus House
Coltsfoot Drive
Peterborough
PE2 9BF
Telephone: 01733 890066
Website: www.youngwriters.co.uk

Book Design by Ashley Janson

Softback ISBN 978-1-80015-698-2

Printed and bound in the UK by BookPrintingUK
Website: www.bookprintinguk.com
YB0490E

FOREWORD

For Young Writers' latest competition This Is Me, we asked primary school pupils to look inside themselves, to think about what makes them unique, and then write a poem about it! They rose to the challenge magnificently and the result is this fantastic collection of poems in a variety of poetic styles.

Here at Young Writers our aim is to encourage creativity in children and to inspire a love of the written word, so it's great to get such an amazing response, with some absolutely fantastic poems. It's important for children to focus on and celebrate themselves and this competition allowed them to write freely and honestly, celebrating what makes them great, expressing their hopes and fears, or simply writing about their favourite things. This Is Me gave them the power of words. The result is a collection of inspirational and moving poems that also showcase their creativity and writing ability.

I'd like to congratulate all the young poets in this anthology, I hope this inspires them to continue with their creative writing.

CONTENTS

The Mount School, York

THE POEMS

This Is Me

Hi, I'm Freya and I love art,
Everything I see goes in my shopping cart,
I usually draw fruit or shapes on my paper,
I'm never bored of art so there is never a later,

I have four pets but they always leave me stressed,
So when I look after them I have to try my best,
I have a hamster, tortoise and two noisy cats,
Who always scratch everything, including all the doormats,

My favourite place is school, however I hate the homework,
I have to finish it or I can't go out,
So I hope I've shared enough because that's what my life is about!
This is me!

Freya Connor (9)
Ashbrook Junior School, Borrowash

This Is Me

When I get home from school I rush upstairs and get changed into my home clothes, and look, collect and sort my trading cards,
When I get home from school I annoy my little brother for fun,
It's fun for him too,
At the weekend I play Roblox for fun,
At lunch and break, I look out for my friends,
And they look out for me,
At school I have a girlfriend, we've been together since nursery,
At home I watched the football, Euro 2020,
My friend is Xander,
My name is Finley,
Often I watch horror movies and sleep downstairs with my awesome rad family,
And my cat and dog.

Finley Gibbons (9)
Ashbrook Junior School, Borrowash

This Is Me

I am a rabbit, cute and cuddly,
I am a cheetah, fast,
I am a horse, super energetic,
I'm an owl, I stay up very late,
I am a monkey, I climb in trees,
I am a bird, free and magnificent,
I'm a puppy, playful and harmless,
I am a pigeon, crazy yet smart,
I am a wolf, hungry and fierce,
I'm as cool as a cucumber,
My hair is as blonde as a Labrador's coat,
My eyes are blue and green like emeralds and diamonds,
This is me!

Arabella Pearson (9)
Ashbrook Junior School, Borrowash

This Is Me

I am...

Tall,
Chocolate eater,
Dancing queen,
Kitten lover,
Best baker,
Doughnut eater,
Book reader,
Grinch watcher,
And dress buyer,

I am a...

D oughnut baker,
I gloo maker,
A nimal lover,
N ice person,
A dvanced person,

L oving,
O rdinary,
B right,
K ind,
O ddly clumsy,
V ery alone,
A nt lover.

Diana Lobkova (9)
Ashbrook Junior School, Borrowash

This Is Me

I have two cats called Moto and Ellie,
I'm creative and artistic,
I like special occasions like parties, Christmas and Halloween,
I'm a baking person and I like baking cooking and biscuits,
I'm sometimes lonely at home or at school,
My favourite drinks are milkshakes and Cokes,
I have one brother and he is three years old,
I have blue eyes like the ocean,
I have pale skin as smooth as cream,
And a friend called JJ,
This is me.

Megan Rees (9)
Ashbrook Junior School, Borrowash

This Is Me

Hey, I'm Lewis and I play football,
And I'm as quick as lightning on a football pitch,
My eyes are as brown as conkers,
And my arms are as hairy as a gorilla,
My dog is my hero and his name is Chase, and he is a boxer dog,
I have a little sister and her hair is as curly as a Curly Whirly,
I am as cool as a lion,
My favourite teachers are Mr Bakewell and Mrs Ward,
I am a pizza fan and that is my favourite food,
This is me.

Lewis Wilson (9)
Ashbrook Junior School, Borrowash

This Is Me

I really like bacon,
But I hate homework,
I am a super-sport kid,
As I do running, cycling, swimming and triathlons,
I have a stuffed toy monkey and a bag of Legos,
Along with an Xbox, family, my bike and a lot of medals,
I also like to read books, play games, play nature and eat,
I like superheroes, friends, snakes, sharks, birds, planes and monkeys,
I am smart and speedy at most things,
This is me.

Tom Pope (9)
Ashbrook Junior School, Borrowash

This Is Me

Good at cricket,
Fast in races,
Master at tactics,
My favourite animal is the dodo,
I would like to be strong,
But it isn't my type,
I am very tall,
A modern man is me,
Technology is my favourite,
I am brave at things when I am afraid of them,
My eyes are brown as copper,
My hair is thick and black,
My favourite place is school,
My hobby will be a teacher,
This is me!

Aroosh Mohammed (9)
Ashbrook Junior School, Borrowash

This Is Me

K ind I am, helpful I am as well,
I am full of energy, see me go,
T ired I am but exhilarated from the day,

F riendly and fancy that's what I am,
E xcited with everything I see from the new, and sometimes through the blue,
A mazing my friends are, and me too,
R usty, I am when I get up in the morning,
N othing can ever dull me, this is me.

Kit Fearn (9)
Ashbrook Junior School, Borrowash

This Is Me

I am a lightning bolt in my trails,
I am a bird, cool and free,
Eyes as blue as the sky,
Hair as green as grass,
I am playful and loving like a dog,
I am a monkey, sticky and funny,
I am a tiger, can be violent, but nice,
I am a sloth, lazy and slow,
I am as strong as a lion,
I am as fast as a really light football,
I'm as nice as a pro football player,
This is me!

Cole Woodland (9)
Ashbrook Junior School, Borrowash

This Is Me

I am a lion cub, cheeky and feisty,
I am a cheetah, fast and bright,
I am as cold as a polar bear,
I am as playful as a cat,
I have eyes as blue as a crystal,
I am as loud as a gorilla,
I'm as hungry as a wolf,
I have hair the colour of clouds,
I'm as strong as a brick house,
I am a wave calm and peaceful,
I am as independent as a math book,
This is me.

Ewan Rigby (9)
Ashbrook Junior School, Borrowash

This Is Me

My hair is blonde and dark,
I like long walks at West Park,
I love to hang out with my friends,
Although we go to school,
This is random but in my sleep, I drool!
I don't get to sleep easy, so I watch TV,
I love to watch anime, nearly every day,
I like board games, books, gym, music and ballet too!
I love my family and cats I really do!
This is me.

Bella Smith (9)
Ashbrook Junior School, Borrowash

This Is Me

L ovely and sweet,
A rtistic and creative,
R espectful and ready,
A mazing and bright,

T all like a tree,
E xtreme and energetic,
R ed is my favourite colour,
Z oom, I am very fast,
O rdinary and normal,
N ice and caring,
I ncredible and excitable.

Lara Terzoni (9)
Ashbrook Junior School, Borrowash

This Is Me

I am a dog, fast and crazy,
I am as cool as a cucumber,
I am brave as a lion,
I am a gamer, king of the PlayStation,
I am as silent as a mouse,
I am as fast as a cheetah,
My eyes are as brown as an oak log,
I am as chatty as a parrot,
I am as fierce as a tiger,
My legs are as powerful as a magic wand,
This is me.

Lucas Reid (10)
Ashbrook Junior School, Borrowash

This Is Me

I am a lightning bolt, fast and strong,
I am a dog, fast and clumsy,
My eyes are as blue as the ocean,
I am a lion, vicious and hairy,
My eyes are as blue as a thunderbolt,
My feet are as small as a mouse,
My hair is as golden as the sun,
I am as suspicious as an imposter,
I am a gamer king of all Xboxes,
This is me.

Leo Swarbrook (9)
Ashbrook Junior School, Borrowash

This Is Me

My name is Sienna,
My eyes are the colour of the ocean,
I am as tall as the Eiffel Tower,
My hair is the colour of conkers,
My lips are as big as an elephant,
My favourite animals are dolphins,
I like going to the park,
I have the best friends ever,
And my favourite place to be is with my family,
This is me.

Sienna Pell (9)
Ashbrook Junior School, Borrowash

This Is Me

I'm a hyena, laughable and fast,
I love drinking apple juice and trust me it never lasts,
My favourite colours are black and red,
I play football, baseball, swimming, karate, rugby and hockey,
My eyes are as brown as Cadbury's chocolate,
I have hair as wavy as the ocean,
I love to binge on Netflix.

Marley Brewin (9)
Ashbrook Junior School, Borrowash

This Is Me

I'm a bird as free as can be,
I'm as cheeky as a monkey,
As loud as a gorilla,
I'm as fast as a cheetah,
I'm a puppy, playful and happy,
My eyes, blue as crystal,
My hair, as brown as land,
As hungry as a wolf,
As good as a monkey,
As cool as a polar bear,
This is me.

Owen Thomas (9)
Ashbrook Junior School, Borrowash

This Is Me

I am a...
Book reader,
Bracelet maker,
Doughnut lover,
Cat queen,
Chocolate eater,
Horse lover,
Goosebumps watcher,
Art maker.

I have,
Two cats,
One older brother,
Soft blonde hair,
Forest-green eyes,
A big smile,
My ears pierced,
This is me.

Amelie Hodgkinson (9)
Ashbrook Junior School, Borrowash

This Is Me

I'm like a monkey, cheeky and happy,
I'm like a sloth, lazy and slow,
I'm a horse scared and glorious,
My hair is golden like the sun,
My eyes are blue like the ocean,
I'm a cat, playful and loving,
I'm cool like a polar bear,
I'm fierce like a lion,
This is me!

Shaya Clarke
Ashbrook Junior School, Borrowash

This Is Me

T all in size,
H elpful,
I 'm artistic and creative,
S ausages are one of my favourite foods,

I have brown eyes like chocolate,
S hy and silly,

M y life is wonderful,
E nergetic that's what I am,

This is me!

Lexie Travers (10)
Ashbrook Junior School, Borrowash

This Is Me

Inside of me is love and kindness,
Inside of me, I will always remember my friends,
Inside of me, I will never forget beauty is on the inside,
Inside of me is joyful when I see white and red roses,
Inside of me, I'm happy when I see my friends are on Roblox,
Inside of me is a caring heart.

Maia Terzoni (9)
Ashbrook Junior School, Borrowash

This Is Me

I'm Winnie the Pooh, hungry and mighty,
I'm a puppy, playful and happy,
I'm an artist, creative and expressive,
My bold crystal-blue eyes like a waterfall at a beauty spot,
I am a vet, loving and caring for all animals,
I am angry, fierce as a lion,
This is me!

Megan Maguire (10)
Ashbrook Junior School, Borrowash

This Is Me

I am a sister to six,
Like a hyena as loud as a newborn chick,
I am a monkey, playful and cute,
My eyes are as brown as mud,
My personality is like a pug,
A thing I like to do is play baseball as well as swimming,
I am 10 years old,
I am mostly cold,
This is me.

Cherry Hayes (10)
Ashbrook Junior School, Borrowash

This Is Me

D arcy is my name, I love my friends and family,
A nimals are one of the things I love like Lego,
R idiculous I can be, but I try not to,
C razy I am and I make people smile,
Y es, I'm kind and helpful to other people.

This is me.

Darcy Smithson Kit (9)
Ashbrook Junior School, Borrowash

This Is Me

I love my family,
I am a friend,
Hair straight like a ruler,
I am as still as a flamingo,
I have a dog, her name is Thorn,
We like to have fun,
I'm as clumsy as a banana,
My room is messy like a cheetah has run through,
This is me.

Maisy Charles (9)
Ashbrook Junior School, Borrowash

This Is Me

J J is my name,
A nd my favourite sport is running,
L earning to go on adventures with my dad,
Y es and I do have a best friend, it's Megan,
N injas is my favourite movie,
N ow it's time to say goodbye.

JJ Towndrow
Ashbrook Junior School, Borrowash

This Is Me

I am as fierce as a wolf,
I am a sloth, lazy and slow,
I'm as cheeky as a monkey with a stolen banana,
I'm as hungry as a lion in the wild,
I'm as playful as a puppy,
My emerald-like eyes shimmer in the sunlight,
This is me!

Beatrix Smith (9)
Ashbrook Junior School, Borrowash

This Is Me

I'm a wave, calm and collected,
I'm a feather, graceful and soft,
I'm as fast as a lightning bolt,
I like yoga, to bend and to stretch,
My eyes shine like a star,
I'm a cheeky monkey, sly and funny,
This is me!

Hannah Lacey (9)
Ashbrook Junior School, Borrowash

This Is Me

I am a cheeky monkey, silly and clumsy,
I am a baby penguin, adventurous and playful,
My hair is as brown as oak wood,
I am a dog, smart and fun,
My eyes are as brown as chocolate,
I am as funny as a clown,
This is me.

Lewis Thompson (9)
Ashbrook Junior School, Borrowash

This Is Me

I am a monkey, cheeky, silly and mega clumsy,
My spaghetti hair flops everywhere,
I am a cat, clingy, loving, cute and fun to play with,
My glowing golden hair shines in the sun,
I'm as messy as my room,
This is me!

Lola Nicholson (9)
Ashbrook Junior School, Borrowash

This Is Me

I am a dog, playful and kind,
Like a puppy with a happy mind,
I am a bird as free as can be,
My eyes are blue like the sea,
My personality is all mixed up,
And I can get told I'm as loud as a duck,
This is me.

Izzabelle Pipes (9)
Ashbrook Junior School, Borrowash

This Is Me

I am a...
Gamer,
Hamster owner,
Pizza eater,
Lego builder,
Kind,
Caring,
Helpful,
Confident,
Brave,
Ice cream devourer,
Talented,
Clumsy,
Fantastic all-rounder,
This is me.

Byron Fox (10)
Ashbrook Junior School, Borrowash

This Is Me

I am kind and loving like a cat,
My eyes are like the ocean,
When I go outside my hair glows like gold in a mine,
I'm happy like a dog,
I am fierce like a lion,
I am as messy as my room,
This is me.

Poppy Smith (9)
Ashbrook Junior School, Borrowash

This Is Me

P asta is my favourite food,
H orses are my favourite animal,
O lives are my favourite side,
E mily is my best friend for life,
B right blue eyes,
E arrings are sparkly.

Phoebe Stirling (9)
Ashbrook Junior School, Borrowash

This Is Me

It was a normal day,
But one unusual night,
I fell off my bike,
I forgot everything,
If you were there you would be blue,
We went to the hospital,
They put gel on my chest,
I could see my heart.

Thomas Hampson (9)
Ashbrook Junior School, Borrowash

This Is Me

I'm a pigeon, lazy and silly,
I'm a fox, playful and sneaky,
I'm as silly as a monkey,
I'm a lover of animals, especially foxes,
I'm as cool as a crisp winter morning,
This is me.

Felix Pearce (9)
Ashbrook Junior School, Borrowash

This Is Me

I'm as friendly as a koala,
I'm as playful as a wild horse,
I'm as lazy as a sloth,
I'm as sweet as sugar,
As bright as the sun,
As cheeky as a cheeky monkey,
This is me.

Harriot Sherlock (9)
Ashbrook Junior School, Borrowash

This Is Me

I am a battle gamer,
I am as silent as a mouse,
Eyes the colour of autumn leaves,
I eat chicken wraps,
I drink cold milk,
I make paper aeroplanes and boats,
This is me!

Logan Foster (10)
Ashbrook Junior School, Borrowash

This Is Me

I am as busy as a bee,
I am a pizza eater,
My hair is like the golden sunshine,
I have a dog called Teddy,
I have a kitten called Buddy,
I like to party,
This is me!

Erin Crampton (9)
Ashbrook Junior School, Borrowash

This Is Me

I am an England football fan,
I am a footballer,
I am a bacon eater,
I am a Fanta drinker,
I am a great gamer,
I have eyes blue like the sea,
This is me!

Jake Biddulph (9)
Ashbrook Junior School, Borrowash

This Is Me

Single gloves are my style,
I play Fortnite all the while,
I like to play with my new kitten,
She is as soft as a mitten.

Niall York (9)
Ashbrook Junior School, Borrowash

This Is Me

Eyes like the blue sea,
Hair as curly as a pretzel,
As cheeky as a monkey,
This is me!

Seth Murfin (9)
Ashbrook Junior School, Borrowash

This Is Me

Marnie Moo,
She is two,
She is my niece
I like to play with her.

Jake Slaney (9)
Ashbrook Junior School, Borrowash

How Covid Made Us Sad

C ovid-19 forced our school to close!
O ver the world, people have died.
R ules were made for us to follow.
O ur family exercised with Joe Wicks!
N urses and doctors were our heroes each day!
A dults wear masks to keep others safe.
V accines are helping us see our family and friends.
I solation was hard and I missed my friends.
R ich or poor the virus did not care...
U s, you and me are safe
S wabs are now part of our life!

Anna Deborah Purce (8)
Ballymagee Primary School, Bangor

The Best School

B allymagee is the best school.
A ll the teachers are very cool.
L iteracy is very fun.
L earning is for everyone.
Y ou always hear the bell ring.
M y favourite subject's everything.
A ssembly is really good.
G orgeous is our canteen food.
E ach day is so fun for me.
E veryone should go to Ballymagee.

Harper Nicholl (8)
Ballymagee Primary School, Bangor

Loving

L oving is a nice thing because God loves all of us.
O ur friends love us like our mums, dads or nannies.
V ery nice people love us because that's who we are.
I think that love is really important and I hope you do too.
N ew people might be born into your family.
G oing to places with your family is really important.

Niamh Campbell (8)
Ballymagee Primary School, Bangor

This Is Me

My smile beams bright and lights up any room.
If I was a cake I'd be hard to bake as I am a sweet little master.
I am quite small but can shout loud and run faster.
I'd be made of strawberries, whipped cream and white chocolate so would look good on any plate.
I want to be a scientist when I grow up.
When I feel sad I think of my mummy and daddy.

Cooper Gray
Ballymagee Primary School, Bangor

Steamies

Follow the tracks
Not looking left, right or back.
Wheels go faster and faster,
Keep control to prevent a disaster.

S team comes out of steam trains.
T homas is a steam train.
E very steamie has a tank for water.
A steamie runs on water and coal.
M useums are great to see steam engines.

Charlie Donnell (8)
Ballymagee Primary School, Bangor

Landings

L oving drums and rhythm sessions.
A eroplanes are really cool!
N o limits to my flying dreams.
D iving, breaststroke in the pool.
I nventing stories with my dad.
N o ball getting in my net.
G reat things, all about me.
S upersonic me? You bet!

Caleb Johnson (8)
Ballymagee Primary School, Bangor

My Chow Chow

R ossi is my chow chow.
O utside he likes to go.
S ometimes in the sunshine.
S ome more times in the snow.
I s he a polar bear in disguise?

Ellise Yates (9)
Ballymagee Primary School, Bangor

This Is Me

In 2020 when I was 9,
I almost got hit by a car!
So let's rewind and tell you how I was almost hit by a car,
So I was riding my scooter down the alleyway,
But then I got too close to the road,
So I squeezed the brake as hard as I could,
And then I stopped at the edge of the road,
And since a car was coming so fast I couldn't see it,
And my hair touched the car.
My heart was racing,
I had never been that scared in my life,
And then I fainted.
About an hour later I woke up in my house,
My mom told me what happened and how I got here.
I went to school the next day,
And this time I didn't ride my scooter.
And that day I learned about road safety,
So when you cross the road, always stop look and listen.

Brody Wickenden (10)
Calmore Junior School, Calmore

There Once Was A Baby

There once was a baby
Who was called Naomi
She was as sweet as can be
She liked to eat chocolate cake
Off of her mummy's plate
And she loved eating chocolate cake with me

There once was a baby
Who was called Naomi
She was as cute as can be
She liked to be tickled
She giggled and wriggled
And she liked being tickled by me

There once was a baby
Who was called Naomi
She was happy as can be
She liked having hugs
And while the adults put coffee in their mugs
She loved having hugs with me

There once was a baby
Who was called Naomi

She was as lovely as can be
Everyone loved her
They kissed and they hugged her
Everyone, especially me!

Grace Piper (10)

Calmore Junior School, Calmore

This Is Me

M y dog is called Bear,
Y oung as a baby he needs lots of care.

P igs are his diet.
E verywhere I go he will follow.
T o get his food we need to handle his mood.

D o lots of training even when it is raining.
O pen a can and he will go for ham.
G oing on a walk will make him talk.

I t is a hard job to cook on the hob when he is overtired.
S oon he will have massive teeth that will be able to rip a leaf.

B igger than most he likes the smell of toast.
E ven though he is hard he gets scared of a bark.
A s well as exhausting it is worth it.
R ussell my uncle likes him, my wonderful Bear.

Maxwell Thorpe (10)
Calmore Junior School, Calmore

This Is Me

What you will need to make your own Dre:

1. A pair of shoes
2. A pound of sugar
3. A hint of cinnamon
4. A bright-coloured hat
5. Six sweet treats
6. A touch of lemon

To start, get a very large bowl,
But make sure that it does not have a hole.
After that add a pound of sugar but not brown,
Because that will make a Dre with a frown.
Add six sweet treats and not six big feet.
Don't forget the touch of lemon - but don't add melon!
Then add a hint of cinnamon.
Mix it together with haste, then leave to rise,
You will know it's done because you will see the eyes.
Slip on a pair of shoes, add a hat - and that's about that!

Dre Young (10)
Calmore Junior School, Calmore

This Is Me

Ingredients:
1 big bag of videogames
A spoonful of happiness
2 small tubs of weirdness
1 bag of respect
10 bags of kindness
20 buckets of shortness
15 bags of annoying.

I'm going to tell you how to make me, this will be easy.
Firstly tip the bag of video games into the bowl,
Add the shortness to the games,
Sprinkle the bag of respect,
Start the mixing.
Pour 15 bags of annoying onto the counter,
Add weirdness, and kindness too,
Start rolling the ingredients, until they make dough,
Add the bowl mixture to the dough,
Bake it in the oven until the cake forms,

Add the sprinkles of happiness, then you're done.
That is me!

Serenity Angel (10)

Calmore Junior School, Calmore

This Is Me

A couple of things about me,
I want to be...
An author and a pro gamer.
My favourite animals are cats!
But I do not like rats!
My zodiac is Taurus bold and brave!
Sweets I really crave!

A couple of things about me...
I have two cats sweet as can be!
Willow is kind of a weirdo,
But sweet and cuddly too!
Shadow is quite a psycho,
And very schizo too!

A couple of things about me...
My friends are as crazy as can be!
I love Pokémon, yes I do,
I love to sing and dance!
I like anime and like to prance,
Now this...
Is me!

Grace Drake (10)
Calmore Junior School, Calmore

My Name Is Hollie

Hi, my name is Hollie, I am very jolly.
One of my hobbies is sewing, my school grades are glowing.
I have a single bunny, I'm not a big fan of honey.
I love Harry Potter,
My second favourite animal is an otter.
My favourite food is crisps,
My least favourite are Skips.
I'm nearly eleven,
My great grandad is in heaven.
My favourite show is My Hero Academia,
If I could change my name I'd change it to Mia.
Thanks for reading my poem,
But I must be going.
Thanks for listening,
Keep your personality glistening.

Hollie Stewart (10)
Calmore Junior School, Calmore

How To Make My Cake

To create my cake you will need:
A love for animals,
A slice of Brownie cake,
10lb of fun and mischief,
A pinch of fun,
A dash of smartness,
A sprinkle of happiness,
A handful of snacks,
And a lot of the sea,
Now you need to:
Add lots of fun and mischief,
Mix in a love for animals.
Stir roughly while adding a slice of Brownie cake,
Next, add a pinch of fun and a dash of smartness,
Spread and mix neatly over a tray of baking powder.
Cook until glazed and fun-filled bubbles can be seen.

Alicia Thorne (10)
Calmore Junior School, Calmore

This Is Me

I have to live with a chocolate eater,
AKA my little sister.
My cats are always fighting over a box,
While my dog is chewing up my socks.

I love to eat pain au chocolate,
I also sometimes enjoy a Mars bar.
I love Starbucks,
But all the cookies suck.

I love my maths,
As much as I love my cats.
I love animals,
And I used to love snails.

The only fruit I like is grapes,
It's so weird I never tried crepes.

This is me Holly and I'm a Leo.

Holly Milton (10)
Calmore Junior School, Calmore

How To Make A Leyton

Ingredients:
One gallon of happiness,
Seven teaspoons of laughter,
One teddy bear,
Four tablespoons of giggles,
Two gallons of coca-cola.
Instructions:
Put one gallon of happiness with a teddy bear, then mix thoroughly,
When it's all foamy add seven teaspoons of laughter, then add one gallon of Coca-Cola,
If it gets watery add four tablespoons of giggles,
Put one more gallon of Coca-Cola then put in the fridge for 24 hours
Now you have a new friend called Leyton.

Leyton Gardner (10)
Calmore Junior School, Calmore

This Is Me

My favourite colour is pastel purple,
I have always loved owls and turtles.
My fantasy is space,
And everyone loves my beautiful face.
In space there are stars,
I'd love to travel to Mars.

I'm artistic, funny and love sports.
You'll probably find me in a swimming pool,
Where it is nice and cool.
I really like riding my bike,
Me and my mum look alike.
I hope you really like me.
I'm just telling you this is all the things I can be!

Lottie Upham (10)
Calmore Junior School, Calmore

This Is Me

I love to wake up early in the morning
Reading books while Mum is still snoring.
I love to run but I'm always number one.
I love to help and am very kind
But don't make me angry at the wrong time.
I love to jump and have fun,
Sometimes I like to watch the sun.
My favourite colour is blue,
Me and my sister love the sunset too.
I love to swim in the cold water,
One day I will swim so fast in the water.
This is me and
I will forever be free.

Trudy Otoo (10)
Calmore Junior School, Calmore

How To Make Me

To make me you will need:
7lb of joy
A dash of anger
50kg of laughter
17kg of calmness
A pinch of sadness
3lb of clumsiness

To begin with, add the pinch of sadness to the 50kg of laughter,
Then mix in 3lb of clumsiness.
You should start to see foam bubbling.
After that add in 17kg of calmness and 7lb of joy.
Now pour into a baking tray and bake for 13 minutes,
Add the dash of anger on top.
Now you have baked yourself me.

Sophie Curtis (10)
Calmore Junior School, Calmore

Excellent Ellie

Hey! I'm Ellie and this is all about me!

I'm not artistic, but I'm funny and sporty,
Some of my friends think I'm dorky.
My favourite colour is pastel purple,
My favourite animals are dogs and turtles.

My favourite subjects are science and maths,
I also have some crazy cats!
I love outer space,
It's the best place.

Yo, I'm sorry, It's the end,
I'm gonna go hang with my lunatic friends.

Ellie-Louise Skeels (10)
Calmore Junior School, Calmore

This Is Me

Things that make me:
Gymnastics - handsprings and cartwheels
Dance - I love twirling
Animals - especially turtles and dogs
Books - my favourite thing is reading
Swimming - I am a water baby
Art - I love being creative
The beach - I'm mainly in the sea the whole time
Turtles - Who doesn't love turtles?
Disney - Tangled is my favourite
Anxiety - I live with it
Autumn - my favourite season
Christmas Eve - my birthday!

Holly Hunt (10)
Calmore Junior School, Calmore

This Is Me

T heme parks are my favourite place to go,
H olidays are my favourite thing to do during the summer,
I love animals.
S wimming is something that makes me happy.

I really would like a dog,
S tranger Things is my favourite series.

M ovies are my favourite thing to watch whilst eating popcorn and sweets,
E ating popcorn and watching a show with my family is something I do often.

Daisy Bull (10)
Calmore Junior School, Calmore

I Love

I love...
Sloths hanging upside down
Books full of adventure
Jacqueline Wilson is my favourite author
Mango with plenty of juice
Puppeteering in the pitch-black
Gymnastics with ribbons
Friends who make me laugh
Family who help me when I need it
Christmas with lots of potatoes
Cheesy pizza with extra cheese
Hot chocolate with a Flake and whipped cream
Drawing pictures from my books
This is me!

Anna Orrey (10)
Calmore Junior School, Calmore

This Is Me

B ook reader,
E nergetic (most of the time)
N ominated school council last year

E ducated at maths,
D iary of a Wimpy Kid are one of my favourite books,
W on a Tom Gates doodling competition,
A mong Us fan,
R ocket League fan too!
D one a lot of weird things in my life...
S cience because I want to become a scientist!

Ben Edwards (10)
Calmore Junior School, Calmore

This Is Me

I am a...
Trampoliner,
Artist,
Scientist,
This is me!
I love my pet she's called Megan.
I love food it's the best,
McDonald's, chocolate and last of all the best sweets!
My favourite game is Fortnite,
My favourite colour is green,
And last of all my favourite subjects are English placing 2nd
And maths placing 1st.
This is me!

Oliver Pascoe (10)
Calmore Junior School, Calmore

How To Make Me

To create me you will need:
Lots of fun and happiness,
Mix in some video games and cheesy balls.
Stir roughly while adding some toughness.
Next, add a pinch of annoyingness
Then spread the mix over a tray neatly on the baking paper,
Cook until glazed and fun bubbles can be seen,
Sprinkle on the happiness and leave to cool down.
This is me!

Aidan Neilson (10)
Calmore Junior School, Calmore

Big George

Yo! The name's Big George,
I got 2k subs and I never rest.
When I grow up I want to be a rock star
Jamming all day and partying all night!
I'll go to different concerts, singing for my fans.
I spend hours and hours on a song
But it's worth it when you can buy everything in gold.
That's it for today, I'll see you tomorrow.

George Dorricott (10)
Calmore Junior School, Calmore

The Slavic Elixir

To create me you will need:

28kg of potatoes,
A splash of holy water,
6 cheburekis,
1 radio,
A slap of linguistics,
And a tad of happiness.

Firstly, add the potatoes,
Then place the cheburekis with some holy water,
Slowly mix in the radio and add the linguistics,
And add a touch of happiness.

Alexander Arnoys (10)
Calmore Junior School, Calmore

My Camera

My camera is called Bob, he is blue.
He is a square camera like all of the others.
I have two cameras but I got Bob for Christmas,
And my other one some time ago.
I can't remember when I got him.
Bob takes pictures of birds and landscapes but he loves hikes.
I am about to get a tripod and climb mountains with Bob.

Theo Brackstone (10)
Calmore Junior School, Calmore

This Is Me

L ovely because I am a lovely friend.
A wesome because I help others when they need it.
U nique because there is no one like me.
R esourceful because I am always ready to make friends.
E xcellent of being a fantastic friend.
N oble to everyone and I help anyone if they're stuck.

Lauren Wyeth (8)
Calmore Junior School, Calmore

This Is Me

J oyful when I spend time with my friends and family.
A mazing at being kind and caring.
D etermined to learn.
A wesome at art, drawing and colouring.

E nergetic when I am doing sports.
Y oung and sporty.
R avenous all the time.
E xcellent at listening.

Jada Eyre (8)
Calmore Junior School, Calmore

All About Me!

I can be weird but caring too.
But when you get to know me I can start to annoy you.
I love Harry Potter, and when I don't read I'm always bored.
I'm very tall but I've got a brain the size of a ping pong ball.
I can be helpful depending on my mood,
But food always fixes my bad mood.

Amy Roberts (10)
Calmore Junior School, Calmore

All About Me

H is for hedgehog because I like hedgehogs.
A is for artistic because I like art.
R is for reliable because you can rely on me.
R is for resourceful because I am great at finding things.
Y is for youngest because I am the second youngest in my family.

Harry Drake (8)
Calmore Junior School, Calmore

This Is Me

M y favourite animal is a panda.
A ffectionate because I like hugs from my family.
G enerous because I like to help when someone is sad.
G reat at maths.
I ntelligent and inquisitive, loves a challenge.
E nthusiastic with learning.

Maggie Clayton-Hart (8)
Calmore Junior School, Calmore

A Poem About Harry

H ilarious because I can cheer people up.
A mazing because I can do things people can't
but it doesn't matter.
R eliable you can trust me to always help you.
R esponsible because I don't mess around.
Y oung because I am not old.

Harry White (8)
Calmore Junior School, Calmore

All About Me

N ice because I like to make others feel happy.
I ntelligent because I like to do extra homework.
A rtistic because I like to paint, colour, sketch and draw things.
M erry because I am always cheerful.
H onest because I tell the truth.

Niamh Cole (8)
Calmore Junior School, Calmore

Things That Make Me, Me!

Gymnastics, I always do this!
Spicy food,
Swimming - I love this,
My brother,
Theme parks - big rides,
Winter,
Disney,
Holidays,
Halloween,
Eating salted popcorn,
Sour Patch Kids - blue and green ones,
My friends!
Ice cream.

Lilly Holmes (10)
Calmore Junior School, Calmore

This Is Me

B eaming, so joyful.
E legant, so graceful.
L ovely, to my friends.
L ively at life.
A mbitious, wants to succeed!

M agnificent, a creature of wonder.
A bundant of joy.
E nchanting, a charmer.

Bella-Mae Watton (8)
Calmore Junior School, Calmore

Animal Lover

A nimal lover.
L ying in bed with my cat and rabbit,
Y awning in the morning when I have to get up,
S miling at my baby rabbit all the time,
S inging to my cat so it can go to sleep,
A lways in my bed with my baby rabbit.

Alyssa Waters (10)
Calmore Junior School, Calmore

This Is Me

T is for thoughtful because I am.
Y ou may not know but I have a little brother.
L oud because I get scared when I jump I scream.
E is for eyes because people say my eyes are beautiful.
R is reliable because I can be relied on.

Tyler Spencer (9)
Calmore Junior School, Calmore

This Is Me

R eliable, I'm there for my friends.
E xcellent at tricks on my scooter.
U nselfish, would give you my last cake.
B rilliant at being cheerful.
E nergetic, I never sit still.
N umber expert, just watch me multiply.

Reuben Barnes (8)
Calmore Junior School, Calmore

This Is Me

C is for cheerful because I am always
H appy.
A is for amazing because I am good at times
table.
R is for rare because I am caring.
L is for loyal because I am king.
I is for intelligent because I like learning.

Charli Reading (8)
Calmore Junior School, Calmore

The Lizard That Travels

R oman the lizard is very mischievous,
O ften he will climb up the curtains and the sofa and
M aybe even the Eiffel Tower!
A fter he might be at the beach. You
N ever know, you might even see my lizard having his tea!

Alfie Saxby (10)
Calmore Junior School, Calmore

Birds

K een on birds,
E njoys watching them,
N est in springtime,
Z ooming into the birds,
O bserving them fighting,

C rows,
R avens,
O wls,
W rens,
E agles maybe.

Kenzo Crowe (10)
Calmore Junior School, Calmore

Lilly

L is for loyal and respectful.
I is for intelligent and loves PE.
L is for lovely and kind because I am kind.
L is for likeable and friendly because I help my friends when they need me.
Y is for yummy and great.

Lilly Osmond (8)
Calmore Junior School, Calmore

This Is Me

B uoyant because I'm full of energy.
R are because my name is unique.
O pen-minded because I have lots of ideas.
D aring because I'll do nearly anything.
Y ounger because I'm the youngest in the class.

Brody Blackburn (8)
Calmore Junior School, Calmore

This Is Me

I am a...
Singer,
Book reader,
Cooker,
Swimmer,
Wasp hater,
Artist,
Early riser,
Cheese and cracker maker,
Light sleeper,
Biscuit eater,
Loves shopping,
And finally,
A kind and helpful person.

Maisie Mills (10)
Calmore Junior School, Calmore

This Is Me

F ortnite is my favourite game,
I deas was a bad idea.
N erds are the best sweets,
D ogs are the best pets,
L ying down is relaxing,
A pples are amazing,
Y ellow is the best colour.

Findlay Newbrook (10)
Calmore Junior School, Calmore

I Am...

I am...
A good friend,
A dog lover,
A good baker,
Good friends with Helen,
Lucky to have good friends,
An artist,
A reader,
A burrito muncher,
Good cousins with Chloe,
Lucky to have good family members.

Evie-Mae Toy (11)
Calmore Junior School, Calmore

This Is Me

T rustworthy at teamwork and being a good friend.
A rtistic at nature art.
R eally want to learn and help people in need.
Y ummy ice cream is my favourite food.
N ice to people so they are kind to me.

Taryn Mould (8)
Calmore Junior School, Calmore

This Is Me

L ike a cheetah,
I love my food, I would go crazy for it.
L ove my pets, just love them so much can't live without them.
L ove the Harry Potter films, I go crazy for them.
Y es, this is me!

Lilly Somerville (10)
Calmore Junior School, Calmore

About Me

J oyful to others.
A wesome football player.
C reative at crafts.
K ind to friends and family.
S uper runner on a track.
O pen-minded at rugby.
N ice to others and pets.

Jackson Payne (9)
Calmore Junior School, Calmore

All About Me

I have a pet that lives on dog treats
And runs like a loony in the living room.
I have a small room
That I have to share with my sister.
I like going to the zoo
Because my favourite animal is there
This is me!

Bella Yeo (10)
Calmore Junior School, Calmore

Joy

Joy lives in the sunniest places
Where all the dreams come true.
But sometimes she bursts out with joy without warning.
Begging to play a game
A new emotion comes bursting,
Anger, as angry as anyone can come.

Isabella Holloway (10)
Calmore Junior School, Calmore

This Is Me

Brown hair (a little bit spiky),
Tall with a big walking stare,
Massive smile and brown eyes,
Always asking questions (always),
Always wants to know more,
I especially don't like writing, especially poems.

Ethan Smith (10)
Calmore Junior School, Calmore

This Is Me

Football is my life it's the only thing I do,
I'd do it in the snow, cold hands, cold fingers,
I don't give a damn.
I want to do it when I'm old enough,
Professional, yes, yes, professional.

George Kneller (10)
Calmore Junior School, Calmore

I Am A...

A kennings poem

I am a...
Harry Potter lover,
Book reader,
Liam Gallagher's music lover,
Plant lover,
Music lover,
Dog lover,
Concert lover,
Autumn lover,
Rain lover,
Guitar lover.

Poppy Durrant (10)
Calmore Junior School, Calmore

This Is Me

A lways analysing at learning.
L oyal classmate.
A rtistic as I love drawing.
I ntelligent, I am a clever girl.
N ever naughty.
A lways an awesome friend.

Alaina Gorfin (8)
Calmore Junior School, Calmore

This Is Me

L oves playing with animals.
A lways up for a challenge.
U pbeat at music.
R esourceful at remembering things.
E xcellent at drawing art.
N ever gives up.

Lauren Griggs (9)
Calmore Junior School, Calmore

This Is Me

G because I am great at basketball.
A because I am amazing at many things.
B because I am brilliant at my times tables.
E because I am energetic at running and
sprinting.

Gabe Knight (8)
Calmore Junior School, Calmore

This Is Me

A for amazing at basketball.
L for loud because that's me.
F for friendly because I cheer people up.
I for incredible at tennis.
E for eager to learn.

Alfie Hanslip (8)
Calmore Junior School, Calmore

This Is Me

I am a...
Animal lover,
A TV watcher,
Love chocolate,
Love shopping for shoes and clothes.
I love my two bunnies and my dog and cat.
I definitely love my family and friends.

Phoebe Weir (10)
Calmore Junior School, Calmore

All About Me

H onest with people.
A mazing at maths.
N ice to everyone.
N ature, I love it.
A rtistic at painting.
H igh spirits for my friends and family.

Hannah Craner (8)
Calmore Junior School, Calmore

This Is Me

H onest to everyone.
A ttentive person.
N oble to my friends.
N ice individual.
A mbitious to do everything in my learning.
H ilarious friend.

Hannah Walton (8)
Calmore Junior School, Calmore

This Is Me

E xcellent at being a friend.
L oyal I'll always be there.
L oves kittens, cute and fluffy.
I maginative.
E xtremely energetic, I do not sit still!

Ellie Mcdonald (8)
Calmore Junior School, Calmore

This Is Me

J ust so you know I'm the only boy in my family.
A lways playing football.
C onsiderate of others.
O utgoing and fun.
B rilliant at building Lego.

Jacob A (8)
Calmore Junior School, Calmore

This Is Me

A kennings poem

I am a...
Superstar,
Kind person,
Helpful person,
Wasp flee-er,
Summer wisher,
Light sleeper,
Early riser,
Book reader,
And finally,
Chocolate eater.

Ella May Gray (10)
Calmore Junior School, Calmore

All About Me

S onny, yesterday my life was filled with rain.
O riginally sunshine.
N atural kid.
N ice person with a fun sense of humour.
Y oung and playful boy.

Sonny Churchill (8)
Calmore Junior School, Calmore

The Boy's Dream

There once was a boy who had a dream,
He wanted to be in the army,
He loved the army, but his mum didn't,
He trained a lot, he wanted to be in the army,
He made wooden guns.

Connor Smith (10)
Calmore Junior School, Calmore

A Poem About Me

L oving with family and friends.
A mazing helper at home and school.
C reative in art.
E nergetic all the time.
Y earning with a drive to succeed.

Lacey Osman (8)
Calmore Junior School, Calmore

A Poem About Harry P

H ilarious and happy.
A mazing and ambitious.
R eliable and safe.
R esourceful and helpful.
Y oung and smart.

P olite and kind.

Harry Pack (8)
Calmore Junior School, Calmore

This Is Me

When I am sad what cheers me up is my dad,
He plays a little sing-song and the sadness is gone.
What also cheers me up is Mia,
My little sister is always there to make me happier.

Izzy Hallett (10)
Calmore Junior School, Calmore

This Is Me

I ntelligent because I am smart
S porty because I like tennis and football.
R are because there is no one like me.
A rtistic because I am good at art.

Isra Abdulaal (8)
Calmore Junior School, Calmore

This Is Me

R eliable and likeable.
O utgoing but very brave.
C aring and a lot of fun.
C reative at stuff.
O riginal but different to other people.

Rocco Darios (8)
Calmore Junior School, Calmore

This Is Me

J oyous, joyful and happy.
A rtistic, good at art.
M arvellous, at doing new things.
E xcellent, at writing.
S uperstar at learning.

James Gawn (8)
Calmore Junior School, Calmore

This Is Me

L oyal and proud of being myself.
E xcellent at reading.
e X traordinary yes I am.
I love my little sister but not so much my brothers.

Lexi Saunders (8)
Calmore Junior School, Calmore

This Is Me

E xcellent, that you're good at something.
R eliable, friend in class.
I maginative, a creative mind.
N ice that you're kind.

Erin Donnelly (8)
Calmore Junior School, Calmore

All About Me

A is for artistic because I create good art.
M is for marvellous because of my handwriting.
Y ou may not know but I have a half brother.

Amy Rose Byrne (8)
Calmore Junior School, Calmore

A Poem About Maya

M erry, abundant joy.
A rtistic, amazing at art projects.
Y earning, a drive to succeed.
A sweet caring girl.

Maya Moseley (8)
Calmore Junior School, Calmore

This Is Me

L istening to music,
E ating,
X box,
I love my dog,
E ating pizza.

Lexie Nash (10)
Calmore Junior School, Calmore

A Poem About Zac

Z appy and happy.
A lways joyful and funny and
C aring and nice.

Zac Gruar (8)
Calmore Junior School, Calmore

Alliterative Me

T hankful, terrific, ticklish.
H appy, helpful, honest.
I ncredible, interesting, inventor.
S ensible, sensational, smart.

I maginative, important, investigative.
S ensitive, special, smiley.

M agnificent, messy, mysterious.
E asy-going, energetic, exciting.

Craig Berrow (11)
Maesteg Comprehensive School, Maesteg

This Is Me

T hinking badly of myself.
H ating myself.
I n a rage.
S ometimes crying.

I nterested in cars.
S upercars are the best!

M anaging emotions.
E very day is a struggle.

Corey Moore (11)
Maesteg Comprehensive School, Maesteg

Considerate Me

T hinking of others.
H elping others.
I nvolving people.
S haring my things.

I ncredible feeling.
S eeing others happy.

M aking friends.
E asy for me.

Sienna Walton (11)
Maesteg Comprehensive School, Maesteg

Shhhhh

T ired always.
H appy in bed.
I n my best place.
S leeping soundly.

I nterrupt me never.
S peak quietly.

M oody am I.
E arly mornings, not for me.

Lincoln Harding (11)
Maesteg Comprehensive School, Maesteg

It's Me, Noah.

T hinking always.
H appy at home.
I n my element.
S laying video games.

I n a KFC bucket.
S cooting about.

M y cat is Sassy.
E veryone likes me.

Noah Jones-Colwell (11)
Maesteg Comprehensive School, Maesteg

Sports Mad

T hrowing javelins.
H urdles I love.
I ncredible speed.
S printing I love.

I nstant glory.
S hiny trophies.

M oving always.
E very sport I love.

Robbie Duncan (11)
Maesteg Comprehensive School, Maesteg

This Is Me

T hrowing netballs.
H appy and free.
I ndependent.
S miling with glee.

I n my element.
S pending time with my dogs.

M any friends.
E mily.

Emily Hevizi (11)
Maesteg Comprehensive School, Maesteg

This Is Me

T eam Titans.
H ero chocolates.
I ncredibles.
S pider-Man.

I ron-Man.
S pongeBob.

M inecraft.
E njoys Lego.

Mckenzie George (11)
Maesteg Comprehensive School, Maesteg

This Is Me

T alented.
H ard-working.
I ntroverted.
S ensible.

I nteresting.
S hy.

M emorable.
E arnest.

Charlotte Fraser (11)
Maesteg Comprehensive School, Maesteg

Sad!

T raumatised.
H elpless.
I nsignificant.
S ad.

I ndifferent.
S trong.

M ournful.
E motional.

Kian Evans (11)
Maesteg Comprehensive School, Maesteg

How To Bake Nayeli

To make me you will need:
979g of kindness.
100g of intelligence.
Lots of homework (not maths)
A handful of happiness.
A pinch of salt.
2 spoonfuls of sugar.
And last but not least,
A science kit.

First, preheat the oven at 180 degrees.
Secondly, add 979g of kindness to a big bowl and mix 100g of intelligence,
Mix until you have a small buttery mixture.
Then in a different bowl, mix a handful of happiness,
Lots of homework, a pinch of sugar and the science kit.
Then put it in the oven for 12 to 18 minutes.
Take out of the oven and enjoy.
This is me.

Nayeli Reid (10)
St George's Primary School, Church Gresley

All About Me!

I like basketball,
I 1v1 them all.
I like video games,
Knock them all off the scoreboard.

I make them fall off their seat,
I am that hard to beat.
As I practise all the time,
Seven days a week.

I'm so good at shooting hoops,
People don't put on their boots.
To come watch me play,
And when I beat a year 11, they all scream, "No way!"

I like eating pizza and pasta,
Whilst watching Oti Mabuse do the cha cha cha.
Or Craig Revel Horwood do the samba,
On Strictly Come Dancing.

This is me!

Zachary Davies (10)
St George's Primary School, Church Gresley

How To Make Me!

Ingredients:
1 teaspoon of forgiveness.
Pinch of sporty.
1 pint of good leadership.
3 gallons of kindness.
5 grams of friendship.
1 gallon of caring.
Jar of honesty.

Firstly, mix one teaspoon of forever forgiveness
And a jar of honesty with the kindest heart.
This should make a condensed paste.
After that, add 5 grams of friendship,
This should look shimmery.
Thirdly add 1 pint of leadership and a pinch of sporty.
Finally add 3 gallons of kindness
And one gallon of caring to make Isabelle.
Leave to cool down.

Isabelle Adams (10)
St George's Primary School, Church Gresley

I Am Me And You Are You

I am happy and funny,
I like chocolate cake.
I love my family,
I play Five-Second Rule, the game, (I lose a lot)
I am clever.

I am amazing.
I read unicorn books.
I enjoy playing with dolls.
I dream to be a unicorn, mermaid and a fairy.

I am helpful.
I try my best.
I want my friends and family to be happy.
I am beautiful.

This makes me, me, and don't be jelly,
Because you are unique too.
And don't think you need to change because of what people think.

Abbey Gibbs (8)
St George's Primary School, Church Gresley

I'd Rather Be Me

I could be a football star,
Or a fast, red and shiny car.
I could be a grey kitten,
Or make snuggly woollen mittens.
I could be an eagle flying high,
Or a courageous astronaut touching the sky.
I could be a builder building houses one by one,
Or a stand-up comedian who tells lots of jokes and puns.
I could be an apple with two seeds beneath my flesh,
Or a riddle-maker leaving people to puzzle and guess.
They all sound great but I have to admit,
I'd rather be me, fabulous wonderful me.

Isobel Gwilliam (10)
St George's Primary School, Church Gresley

This Is Me

You will need:

A drop of kindness.
A tub full of craziness.
A jug of clumsiness.
A years supply of laziness.
A pinch of energeticness and helpfulness.
A box full of smartness.

First, add a drop of kindness.
Next a tub full of craziness.
Third a jug full of clumsiness.
After that, a year's supply of laziness.
A pinch of energeticness and helpfulness,
And finally a box of smartness.
Now mix, then put in a cooking tray.
Then let it cool.

Olivia Sophia Cook (10)
St George's Primary School, Church Gresley

Me

R ed is my favourite colour.
E xcellent is me.
E very time I'm ready
C ool is me.
E veryone likes me.

A football is my thing.
L ove is my family.
E veryone that is my friend is the best.
X -ray scans help you.
Z ebras are great animals.
A bee helps you.
N ice people help you.
D ead people were good.
E veryone is your best friend.
R eece is my name.

Reece Pollard (8)
St George's Primary School, Church Gresley

Marvellous Me

The first thing you have to know about me,
Is that I love roller coasters and to watch TV.

I play bass in a rock 'n' roll band,
So blisters are popping up on my hand.

I love food like garlic bread,
I don't like veg, I'll have sweets instead.

My favourite place is Alton Towers,
I don't smell since I have lots of showers.

I support the team Aston Villa,
And just one last thing and it's that I'm a gamer.

George Elwyn Weighall (10)
St George's Primary School, Church Gresley

Make Me!

Things to make a star cookie! (Me!)
A pinch of laziness, a big cup of respect and a teaspoon of caring powder!
Sprinkles of happiness.
Friendliness dough.
A warm cosy oven, and a star cookie cutter!

How to make it! (Me!)
Get a cup of respect, a teaspoon of caring powder and a pinch of laziness.
Mix the dough and cut using the star cookie cutter.
Bake in the oven and put the sprinkles on, and done!

Well done! You made a star cookie... me!

Olivia Smith (10)
St George's Primary School, Church Gresley

When I Was Not Me

I am me, always was, always will be.
Happy, humorous, excited, exotic that's who I am.
Specific, concentrating, clever that's me!

Fast, scary and sometimes bored, that's who I am.
But then I was not happy, not humorous, not excited, not exotic,
That's not who I am.

Not specific, not concentrating, not clever, that's not me.
Not fast, not scary and not bored.
That's not what I should be.
Because that's not me.

Elijah Hackett (8)
St George's Primary School, Church Gresley

The One And Only Me

I am a fox, cunning and sly,
I live life, I never say die.

I am sporty, fit and energetic,
But when I stop, I have a need to fidget.

I rather like it when it snows,
But when it will, I'll never know.

I am kind, honest and loyal at heart,
But I can never stop only start.

I have grey eyes and long brown hair,
But when there are maths tests, I really don't care.
I am the one and only me.

Matthew Ball (10)
St George's Primary School, Church Gresley

All About Me!

I'm as cool as a skeleton.
I like playing My Singing Monsters as much as Minecraft.
I am not a nerd as you just heard, I'm just average and so are you.
You're all special and so I am too.
I have got an endangered species of pets,
But they don't really go to the vets.
Why does this sound like a rap?
I don't know but I'm not turning on the tap.
Do you know the size of my fist?
It's the size of mist.

Harry Cheshire (8)
St George's Primary School, Church Gresley

The Meaning Of Me!

I am into dancing,
When I go home I like to do a little prancing.

I am full of excitement and a chatterbox,
I have great eyesight like a fox.

I am as funny as a mischievous monkey,
I can be sassy and very funky.

I am as loving as a pumping heart,
I enjoy learning and I'm quite smart.

I am fun and very cheerful,
I put smiles on people's faces and I'm never dull.

This is me!

Maisie Bailey (10)
St George's Primary School, Church Gresley

Me!

This is me!
She can't be me, he can't be me.
I am unique!

Being me means gaming, music, family.
Craziness is me too.
Being me is both hard and fun.

I love food that's me too.
Don't be jealous of me because you're unique and amazing too.

I love being me and that's why I'm me.
I don't know what I want to be but for now, I'll be kid me.

That's me!

Sadé Taylor (8)
St George's Primary School, Church Gresley

I Am Samuel Batten

S uper smart.
A mazingly kind person.
M aking delicious carrot cake.
U sing tubes to make rice shakers, I am creative.
E xcellent writer.
L oving and caring.

B anging brother.
A ngry sometimes.
T alking a lot.
T rying not to cry.
E ven if it hurts I can keep it in.
N ever mind I still love my brother.

Samuel Batten (8)
St George's Primary School, Church Gresley

I'm A Panda!

I am a panda!
I have sooty black spots all over,
And feed all day.
I eat big green tubes,
Known as bamboo.
It's also used as scaffolding,
In a certain part of the world.
My species is endangered,
Even though we hide in reserves.
People call us good-for-nothing,
But not as much as koalas.
I lounge around all day,
But I'm still quite productive.
I am a panda!

Sebastian Whiten (10)
St George's Primary School, Church Gresley

All About Me

I am a pleasant girl,
I like playing with friends,
I love my family,
I play in the garden,
I am kind to everyone,
I am helpful to everyone,
I read lots of books,
I enjoy going to the park,
I am always happy,
I am good at listening,
I pretend to be a mummy,
I try to be at school,
I want to be a teacher when I'm big,
I am good at doing the splits.

Mariah Adekoya (8)
St George's Primary School, Church Gresley

Acrostic Me!

W icked as a witch,
I ndependent as a small quiet mouse,
N oisy as an elephant,
N aughty as a monkey,
I ntelligent as a cat,
E motive as a snake.

W ary as a panda,
I neffective as a bear,
L ight as a frog,
S elective as a dog,
O rganised as a hamster,
N ice as a gerbil.

Winnie Wilson (8)
St George's Primary School, Church Gresley

Who Am I?

I am a mammal of the land.
I do not live near any sand.

I am a smart little thing.
But I can't sing.

My voice is heard from all around.
And I like to make a lot of sound.

I am a kind and loyal friend.
And my legs never end!

I like to think of myself as funny.
And my words are as sweet as honey.
Who am I?
I am me!

Holly Forrest (10)
St George's Primary School, Church Gresley

This Is Me, Only About Me!

I am as calm as a panda.
I am as caring as a nurse.
I am as confident, strong and brave as a lion.
I am as shy as a snail.
I am as hard as a turtle's shell.
I am as helpful as 999.
I am as tall as a giraffe.
I am as perfect as a smooth marble.
I am as bright and colourful as a dolphin.
Last but not least I am me, I am unique, no one can change that.

Maisy Autumn Brooks (10)
St George's Primary School, Church Gresley

This Is Me

I am funny,
I like chocolate,
I love my family,
I play Roblox,
I am clever.

I am happy,
I read animal books,
I enjoy playing with my family,
I dream if I could be a fairy,
I am helpful.

I am me,
I try my best,
I want a big doll,
I help my friends and family,
I am good at playing games.

Do not be jel!

Lilly Hines (8)
St George's Primary School, Church Gresley

This Is Me!

T he funny side of me can show when I want.
H aving my friends is the best of fun.
I am as loyal as a guard cat.
S trong but silent.

I am as sensitive as a mouse.
S cience, crazy about the human body.

M y hair and eyes are as brown as bark.
E veryone can be them, but I want to be me.

Amelia Morton (10)
St George's Primary School, Church Gresley

What I Am

I am as determined as a champion,
but as brave as a lion.
I am very funny,
and also silly.

I am as scared as a fox,
but I don't hide in a box.
I am as warm as the sun,
but as cold as ice.

I'm as royal as a queen,
but as buzzed as a bee.
I am a football lover,
there is a lot of stuff to discover.

Joshua Earp (10)
St George's Primary School, Church Gresley

This Is Me

I am a Lamborghini on the pitch,
I am a determined defender,
I am energetic like Mo Farah,
I am a black panther, hard-working and brave,
I am sporty like Cristiano Ronaldo,
I am as funny as a monkey,
My eyes are ocean blue marbles,
My hair waves at sea,
My ears are as sensitive as an elephant's.

This is me!

Oscar James Clamp (11)
St George's Primary School, Church Gresley

Mystery Mammal!

My animal is...
A very intelligent species,
Is a friendly swimmer,
Can do amazing tricks,
Has ocean blue skin,
Can beat lightning in a race,
Makes noise when calling others,
Is a sea mammal,
Has many fishy friends,
Gives people wet kisses,
Protester for no litter.
What am I?

Answer: A dolphin.

Evie Davies (10)
St George's Primary School, Church Gresley

All About Me

I am good,
I like my family,
I love going on holiday,
I play outside in the garden,
I am helpful to my family,
I am always nice to everyone,
I read,
I enjoy my life,
I am funny,
I am smart,
I pretend to be a footballer,
I try my best in school,
I want some Christmas presents,
I am very excited.

Elijah Adekoya (8)
St George's Primary School, Church Gresley

This Is Me

I am happy and kind,
I like dogs and cats,
I love maths,
I play with my brother and sister,
I am clever,
I am funny,
I read school books,
I enjoy maths,
I dream of being a YouTuber,
I am amazing,
I am helpful,
I pretend with my sister,
I try my best,
I want to be a dancer,
I am friendly.

Darcie-Mae O'Kelly (8)
St George's Primary School, Church Gresley

Who Am I In The World?

As wild as I can be,
Yet civilised and smart.

Hair the colour of oak,
Yet wavy like the calm sea.

Playful as a pup,
Clumsy as a kitten.

My birth year, a tiger,
But very nearly not.

My eyes are like part of a rainbow,
What exact colour, I do not know.
Who am I?

Jessica Morritt (10)
St George's Primary School, Church Gresley

All About Me

I am kind.
I like to read.
I love my dog.
I play Roblox.
I am a genius.
I am helpful.
I read Alex Rider.
I play Lego.
I dream about being nice.
I am funny.
I am fantastic.
I pretend to be a policeman.
I try to get stronger.
I want a fake minigun.
I am big and strong.

Conall Hollender (8)
St George's Primary School, Church Gresley

All About Me

I'm crazier than a monkey,
I'm softer than a baby duck,
I'm harmless like a bunny,
I swim better than a fish,
I am stronger than a rhino,
I am braver than a lion,
I am funnier than a bird,
I am faster than a cheetah,
I am pretty in pink like a flamingo,
I'm cosy like a bear.

Hermione Potts (8)
St George's Primary School, Church Gresley

I Am...

I am...
As bright as the sun,
As calm as a diver,
As brave as a bear,
As fast as a hare,
As mischievous as a monkey,
As colourful as a rainbow,
As shy as a mole,
As clumsy as a foal,
As friendly as a dog,
As thoughtful as a turtle,
I am all those things...
And I am me!

Phoebe Leah Felthouse (10)
St George's Primary School, Church Gresley

This Is Me

I am as funny as a monkey who laughs all day!
I am as brave as a lion who works alone,
I am a kind and helpful little kitten,
I am as fast as a cheetah when I play football,
I am an animal lover who has an unbreakable friendship bond,
I am a friendly little tiny mouse, who will give you no harm.

Chelsey Jerome (10)
St George's Primary School, Church Gresley

This Is Me!

M e as quiet as a mouse.
A nd my ears you can hear so good.
D o a somersault which I can do.
I scream so loud I will wake you.
S o I can see so well I can see like a fox.
O n the weekend I do fun stuff.
N o one can be me except for me.

Madison Colarelli (8)
St George's Primary School, Church Gresley

I Am Me

I like to help people, I like playing games.
I want to be a footballer, I want to be a YouTuber.
I want to be a lot of things.
I like to eat. I like to eat many things.
I like many things.
Brown bears, jumping jaguars and slimy snakes.
What do you know about me?
I am me.

Archie Bonser (8)
St George's Primary School, Church Gresley

All About Me

I am funny, I like games.
I love maths, I play Fortnite.
I am amazing.
I am fantastic.
I read Avengers.
I play with my friends.
I love being a footballer.
I am kind.
I am fantastic at maths.
I try to eat new food.
I want a new trampoline.
I am great.

Blake Glover (8)
St George's Primary School, Church Gresley

All About Me

I am very happy,
I like Fortnite,
I love puppies,
I play superheroes,
I am cool.

I am funny,
I read Roald Dahl books,
I enjoy burgers,
I dream to be a YouTuber,
I am wonderful.

I am scary,
I pretend to be Venom,
I try to win.

Oliver Bowater (8)
St George's Primary School, Church Gresley

This Is Me!

I am as gentle as a newborn kitten,
I am as loyal as a whale,
I am courageous like a clouded leopard,
I am as playful as a puppy,
I am an animal lover,
I am a reader,
My hair is like a red rose,
My eyes are like the ocean,
I am tiny in size,
This is me!

Michaela Alexander (10)
St George's Primary School, Church Gresley

This Is Me

I am a team player,
Resourceful with every touch,
I am active and can play the full match,
I perceiver when we are losing,
Like a bomb when I shoot,
The football pitch is my real home,
Finally where I belong,
The thing I love doing, in the palm of my hand.

Oscar Edwards (10)
St George's Primary School, Church Gresley

This Is Me

I am helpful.
I love playing Xbox.
My favourite colour is blue.
This is me.

I am cool.
I love gaming.
My favourite food is McDonald's.
This is me.

I am kind.
I love Coca-Cola.
My favourite colour is black.
This is me.

Lucas Dooner (8)
St George's Primary School, Church Gresley

Me!

This is me and what I love.
I am always ready to learn,
I like playing with my sister,
I like reading my book,
I have fun drawing art and English,
I like being crazy at home,
I like the Romans so far in topics,
I like running around and being energetic.

Georgia Jones (9)
St George's Primary School, Church Gresley

The Gaming Poem

I like Fortnite that's what I do,
I go swimming that's fun for me.
I try my best at everything I do that's me,
I like takeaways, hot dogs, McDonald's and pizza.
I like Roblox, FNF and Sorcerer Fighting Simulator.
I am my family,
This is me.

Oliver McCormick (8)
St George's Primary School, Church Gresley

We Are Kind

I am kind and helpful with a smile on my face.
You will find me playing football on the field with my friends.
I love planting vegetables and sunflowers with my dad.
Reading is important and fun.
I do it every day, I am happy and cheerful.
I love being me.

Ruben Pykitt (8) & Matthew Clarke (8)
St George's Primary School, Church Gresley

This Is Me

E ntertaining for others,
V ery kind,
E ager to learn,
L oves everyone,
Y oung,
N ever boring.

R andom,
E njoyable,
I mpressive towards others,
D ecent.

Evelyn Reid (8)
St George's Primary School, Church Gresley

This Is Me

I am brave, like a roaring lion.
I am calm, like a baby panda.
I am as intelligent as a shining blue dolphin.
I am as creative as a bright red robin.
I am as thoughtful as a star shining bright in the night sky.

This is me.

Makayla Avah Foster (10)
St George's Primary School, Church Gresley

What Am I?

I am big,
I am scary,
I love meat yum,
I love hiding,
I love sleeping,
I love to chase my prey,
I like to make noise,
But I don't like to play with toys.
What am I?

Answer: A lion.

Skye Cuthbert (10)
St George's Primary School, Church Gresley

What Am I?

I love to play games and have fun,
I love carrots, they are yum in my tum.
My mum clears me out every week,
I play, I stay but I don't go away.
I like to sleep.
What am I?

Answer: A bunny rabbit.

Tianna Gutteridge (11)
St George's Primary School, Church Gresley

Ancient Reptilian Riddle

I am loyal to my pack (my family and friends).
I am brave and will try new things.
I am patient and I will wait if I have to.
I am smart.
I am a dinosaur fan.
What am I?

Answer: A velociraptor.

Ruqayya Alexandra (10)
St George's Primary School, Church Gresley

This Is Me

I am a lightning bolt in football boots,
I'm a superstar striker.
I am a panther because I am brave,
My eyes are very blue like a marble.
I score every week,
I love my friends and family.

Oliver-Jack Grime (10)
St George's Primary School, Church Gresley

Football

F avourite colour is black.
O wns a skateboard.
O verexcited.
T oo crazy.
B ad at English.
A mazing.
L oves football.
L oves gaming.

Dylan Morritt (8)
St George's Primary School, Church Gresley

I Love My Kittens

I love my kittens,
They are fluffy, funny and fast,
They make me feel happy and calm,
They're playful, jumpy and chasy,
They're sleepy, cuddly and cute,
I love my kittens.

Louie Baker (9)
St George's Primary School, Church Gresley

This Is Me

M y life is special,
A nd I am funny as a kitten.
K ind as possible,
S ometimes,
I am myself.
M any people are themselves.

Maksim Ksenofontovs (8)
St George's Primary School, Church Gresley

All About Me

J ogging in the park.
A bout to play Fortnite.
C ake in the kitchen.
O n Monday I go to school.
B ut all I love is my family.

Jacob Taylor (8)
St George's Primary School, Church Gresley

This Is Me

This is me,
I am kind,
I like colouring,
I like playing on the PS4,
I am clever,
I want to be like my dad when I grow up.
That is me.

Benjamin Pekacet (9)
St George's Primary School, Church Gresley

This Is Me

R eady to learn.
I ncredible at science.
L oves my family.
E xcellent friend.
Y ear 4.

Pantall (9)
St George's Primary School, Church Gresley

Me

I am ambidextrous.
I am cool.
I am fast.
I am good at football.
I am a good gamer.
I am good at maths.

Harry Dolman (8)
St George's Primary School, Church Gresley

How To Make: Me

To create me you will need:
A snuggle of sloths
A handful of books
120g of positive thoughts
A gift of kindness
A well of friendship
A pinch of patience
An endless supply of loyalty
A tub of thoughtfulness
A bowl full of cake mixture
Now you need to:
Add a tub of thoughtfulness.
Next mix in a handful of books and a pinch of patience then stir well.
Add your endless supply of loyalty.
Then fold in a gift of kindness and a well of friendship.
Now carefully add in the snuggle of sloths.
Put in the oven for one hour,
Then sprinkle on your 120g of positive thoughts.
And there it is: Me.

Melanie Stott (10)
The Mount School, York

A Milkshake Of Me

To create me you will need:
A bookshelf of murder mysteries
101 books on how to draw anime
A pair of rollerskates
10lbs of Japanese stationery
A sprinkle of happiness

Now you need to:
Mix the pair of rollerskates with the 10lbs of Japanese stationery together, until a periwinkle blue.
Fold in the murder mysteries and sprinkle in the happiness, now the mixture should be lilac.
Add the 101 books on how to draw anime, watch as it bubbles and finally turns glittery.
Pour in a glass and drink!
This is me!

Edith Silver-Gilmore (10)
The Mount School, York

How To Make A Me!

Ingredients:
Take a cup of sass,
A pinch of spice,
3 teaspoons of fun,
A world full of unicorns,
3 different sparkly pink colour palettes,
A sprinkle of happiness.

Now you need:
To start with a world full of unicorns,
Then add half cup of sass,
3 teaspoons of fun,
A pinch of spice,
3 different sparkly pink colour palettes,
And finally, on top, a sprinkle of happiness!
This is me!

Eleanor Fryer (10)
The Mount School, York

A Recipe For Me

To create me you will need:
A brightly coloured bedroom.
A bowl of rice with tuna.
A colourful pair of earrings.
A light sunshine.
A chocolate and orange cake.
A stable full of horses.
A sprinkle of positivity.
A package of happiness.
A beautiful violin.
A bottle full of mango juice.
A 100g of an enchanting mindset.
A shop full of Tamagotchis.
This is me.

Francesca Bastardo (9)
The Mount School, York

I Am

A kennings poem

I am a...
Friend supporter
Person helper
Problem solver
Book reader
Frida Kahlo follower
Monkey enthusiast
Mouse lover
Creative writer
Gymnastics do-er
Cake scoffer
Good singer
Pancake adorer
And finally...
I am me!

Agnes Obi (9)
The Mount School, York

Me!

Me, a kind loving soul,
Me, singing all the time,
Me, bouncing up and down,
Me, eating Lindt chocolate galore,
Me, loud and proud,
Me, clonky feet,
Me, a massive pizzaholic,
Me, the best I can be!

Isabelle Evington (11)
The Mount School, York

YoungWriters Est. 1991

YOUNG WRITERS INFORMATION

We hope you have enjoyed reading this book – and that you will continue to in the coming years.

If you're the parent or family member of an enthusiastic poet or story writer, do visit our website **www.youngwriters.co.uk/subscribe** and sign up to receive news, competitions, writing challenges and tips, activities and much, much more! There's lots to keep budding writers motivated!

If you would like to order further copies of this book, or any of our other titles, then please give us a call or order via your online account.

Young Writers
Remus House
Coltsfoot Drive
Peterborough
PE2 9BF
(01733) 890066
info@youngwriters.co.uk

Join in the conversation!
Tips, news, giveaways and much more!

YoungWritersUK YoungWritersCW youngwriterscw